HORSING AROUND

APPALOOSAS

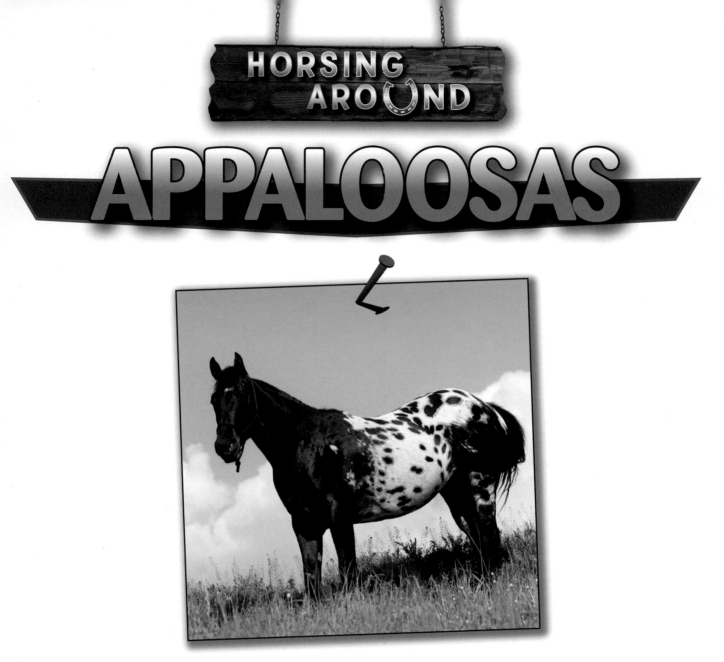

By Barbara M. Linde

Gareth Stevens
Publishing

Please visit our website, www.garethstevens.com. For a free color catalog of all our high-quality books, call toll free 1-800-542-2595 or fax 1-877-542-2596.

Library of Congress Cataloging-in-Publication Data

Linde, Barbara M.
Appaloosas / Barbara M. Linde.
     p. cm. — (Horsing around)
Includes index.
ISBN 978-1-4339-6458-9 (pbk.)
ISBN 978-1-4339-6459-6 (6-pack)
ISBN 978-1-4339-6456-5 (library binding)
1. Appaloosa horse—Juvenile literature. I. Title.
SF293.A7L56 2012
636.1'3—dc23

2011020895

First Edition

Published in 2012 by
Gareth Stevens Publishing
111 East 14th Street, Suite 349
New York, NY 10003

Copyright © 2012 Gareth Stevens Publishing

Designer: Michael J. Flynn
Editor: Therese Shea

Photo credits: Cover, p. 1, (cover, back cover, p. 1 wooden sign), (front cover, pp. 2–4, 6, 8, 11, 12, 15, 16, 19–24, back cover wood background), pp. 4–6, 7 (all), 13–14, 17 Shutterstock.com; p. 9 Prehistoric/The Bridgeman Art Library/Getty Images; pp. 10, 18 Marilyn Angel Wynn/Nativestock/Collection Mix: Subjects/Getty Images.

Printed in the United States of America

CPSIA compliance information: Batch #CW12GS: For further information contact Gareth Stevens, New York, New York at 1-800-542-2595.

Contents

Words in the glossary appear in **bold** type the first time they are used in the text.

What Is an Appaloosa?

Have you ever seen a horse with a spotted coat? It was probably an Appaloosa! This **breed** of horses has stripes on its hoofs and a short mane and tail.

An Appaloosa is usually between 14 and 16 **hands** high. This is between 56 and 64 inches (142 and 163 cm) tall.

Most horses have large dark eyes. However, Appaloosas have a white **sclera** surrounding each iris, or colored part of the eye—just like people do.

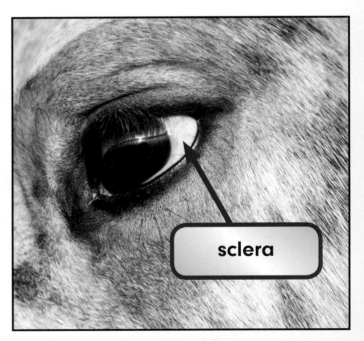

sclera

A horse's height is measured at the highest point of its shoulders, which is called the withers.

All Appaloosas have **mottled** skin. This means some patches of skin are dark, while others are pinkish. The Appaloosa is the only horse that has this mottled skin.

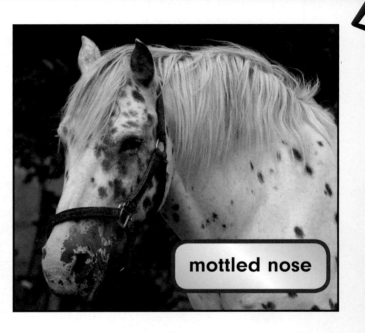

mottled nose

Not all Appaloosas have spotted coats. An Appaloosa can have one coat pattern or a mix of coat patterns. Its coat might be a solid color, too. Coat patterns may change as horses get older. Look on the next page to read some terms for coat colors and patterns and to see what they look like.

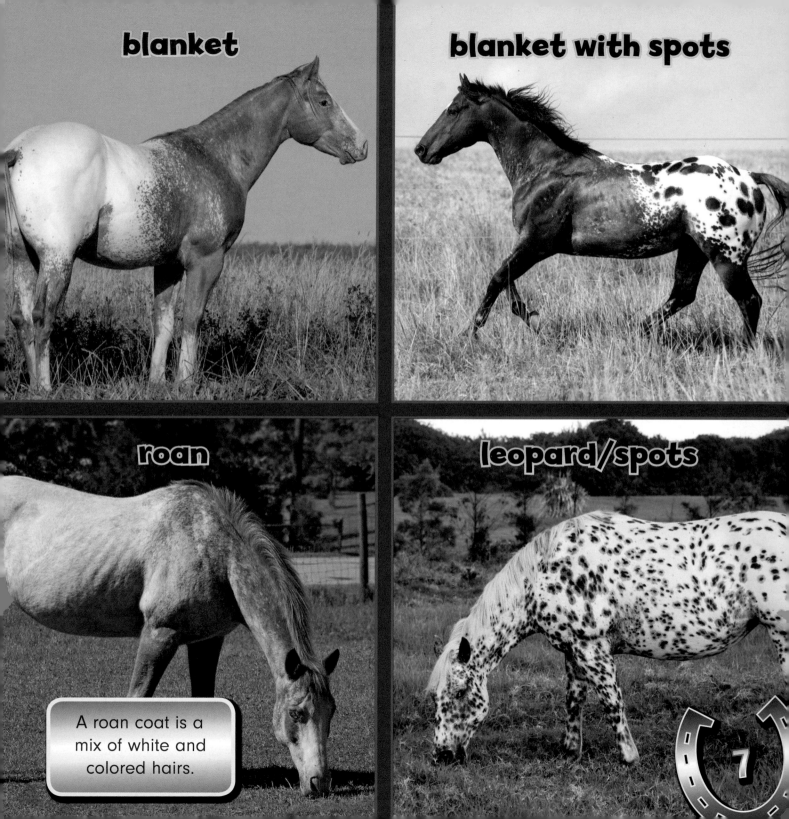

blanket

blanket with spots

roan

leopard/spots

A roan coat is a mix of white and colored hairs.

7

Spotted horses have been around since ancient times. Some are featured in cave paintings in Spain that date back over 20,000 years. The Chinese have passed down ancient stories of spotted horses from heaven. Ancient Greek pottery also features spotted horses. The Persians claimed the very first spotted horse was a powerful warhorse called Rakush who lived around 400 BC.

Years later, in Europe, royalty often chose to ride spotted horses. In the 16th century, Spanish explorers brought the first modern horses to North America, including spotted ones.

These prehistoric paintings of spotted horses were found in southern Spain in a cave called Cueva de la Pileta.

THE MANE FACT

Early horses lived in North and South America about 3 million years ago, then died out. There weren't any other horses in the Americas until Spanish explorers brought them.

9

Native Americans found that Appaloosas were good at hunting buffalo. The horses were fast and unafraid of the big animals.

THE MANE FACT

White settlers called the Native Americans' spotted horses "Palouse horses" after the Palouse River in the Northwest. This name later changed to "Appaloosa."

The early Spanish explorers introduced horses to Native Americans in the American Southwest. Over time, horses spread to tribes in other areas. The Nez Perce in the Northwest began raising horses. Explorer Meriwether Lewis noted the beauty of the tribe's many spotted horses in his writings. Around the early 1800s, these spotted horses became known as Appaloosas.

Horses changed the Nez Perce way of life. Once fishermen, they became hunters and traders. However, in the late 1800s, the Nez Perce lost a war against the US government. Their horses were taken away.

The Return of the Appaloosa

After the government took away the Nez Perce horses, Appaloosas became uncommon. However, as some began to be used in western shows and **rodeos**, their colorful spotted coats drew people's interest.

In 1937, Francis Haines wrote an article about Appaloosas for *Western Horseman* magazine. It started a new interest in the breed. In 1938, a group formed the Appaloosa Horse Club. More people began raising Appaloosas. Today the Appaloosa is a well-known and popular breed.

THE MANE FACT

The Appaloosa Horse Club has kept records of over 700,000 Appaloosas since 1938.

Appaloosas are good rodeo horses because they're easy to train and are hard workers. This horse and rider are taking part in a cattle-roping event.

13

Many Appaloosas are skilled in English-riding events such as show jumping.

THE MANE FACT

The Appaloosa became the official state horse of Idaho in 1975.

14

Not all Appaloosas have the same kind of body. Their different bodies make them good at different tasks. Some heavy Appaloosas are used to do ranch work, such as herding cattle. However, they're not usually used to pull farm wagons or do other kinds of hard work. Some Appaloosas are tall and thin. They do well in certain races and as show horses.

There have even been a few Appaloosas in Hollywood! They're featured in many movies about the Old West. Since Appaloosas are easy to train, they make good acting horses.

Appaloosas are excellent horses for those learning to ride and for trail riding. Every year, the Appaloosa Museum in Idaho has a trail ride on the land of the Nez Perce.

People who love Appaloosas join groups for fun and for **competition**. The Appaloosa Horse Club has shows and other events for riders of all ages. The Appaloosa Youth **Association** has art, photo, and writing contests. It offers special events for young people with disabilities. The association also helps young riders compete in other countries.

THE MANE FACT

There are Appaloosa clubs in over 20 countries, including Sweden, Switzerland, South Africa, Mexico, Israel, and Brazil.

Appaloosas are often described as easygoing as well as easy to train.

Many Nez Perce had never ridden a horse before the Young Horseman Project.

Many Nez Perce now live on a **reservation** in Lapwai, Idaho. A few years ago, businessmen gave the tribe four Akhal-Teke **stallions** from Central Asia. The tribe used these horses and Appaloosa **mares** to begin a new breed called the Nez Perce horse. This breed is thought to be much like the Nez Perce Appaloosas of the 1800s.

The Nez Perce also started the Young Horseman Project for young people. The project honors these Native Americans' way of life while giving young people opportunities to learn about horses.

Like all horses, Appaloosas need food, water, and exercise. They should see a **veterinarian** for regular checkups and teeth cleaning. They can easily catch an eye **disease** that's sometimes called moon blindness. If the problem isn't treated properly, the horse can go blind.

Appaloosas can sunburn, especially on the pink areas of their mottled skin. Some veterinarians suggest sunscreen and shade. Healthy Appaloosas, with their eye-catching coats and interesting history, are sure to remain some of the best-loved horses.

THE MANE FACT

Some Appaloosas are born with night blindness. It's hard for them to see at night or in low light.

The Appaloosa Timeline

around 18,000 BC	Spotted horses are featured in cave paintings.
1500s	Spotted horses arrive in the Americas.
1800s	Spotted horses are named Appaloosas.
1877	Appaloosas are taken away from the Nez Perce.
1938	The Appaloosa Horse Club forms.
1995	The Nez Perce horse breed begins.
2011	More than 700,000 records of Appaloosas have been collected by the Appaloosa Horse Club.

Glossary

association: a group of people joined together for a purpose

breed: a group of animals that share features different from other groups of the kind

competition: the process of trying to win or do something better than others

disease: illness

hand: a measurement used for a horse's height. One hand equals 4 inches (10.2 cm).

mare: an adult female horse

mottled: having patches or spots of different colors

reservation: land set aside by the US government for Native Americans

rodeo: an event in which people compete using cowboy skills

sclera: the white part of the eyeball

stallion: an adult male horse

veterinarian: a doctor who is trained to treat animals

For More Information

Books

Criscione, Rachel Damon. *The Appaloosa.* New York, NY: PowerKids Press, 2007.

Yerxa, Leo. *Ancient Thunder.* Berkeley, CA: Publishers Group West, 2006.

Websites

Appaloosa
www.ansi.okstate.edu/breeds/horses/appaloosa/
Read a brief history of the Appaloosa.

The Appaloosa Museum and Heritage Center Foundation
www.appaloosamuseum.org
Plan a visit to the Appaloosa Museum.

Appaloosa Youth Association
www.appaloosayouth.com
Learn more about Appaloosas and their young riders.